Going Skiing
Coloring Book For Kids

Cute Animals & Children Doing Winter Sports
Cold Season Colouring for Ages 4-8

Rachel Mintz

Thank You for coloring with us - Going Skiing!

Here are some extra coloring pages from our book 'Summer Fun', if you like them you can find the book at Amazon.

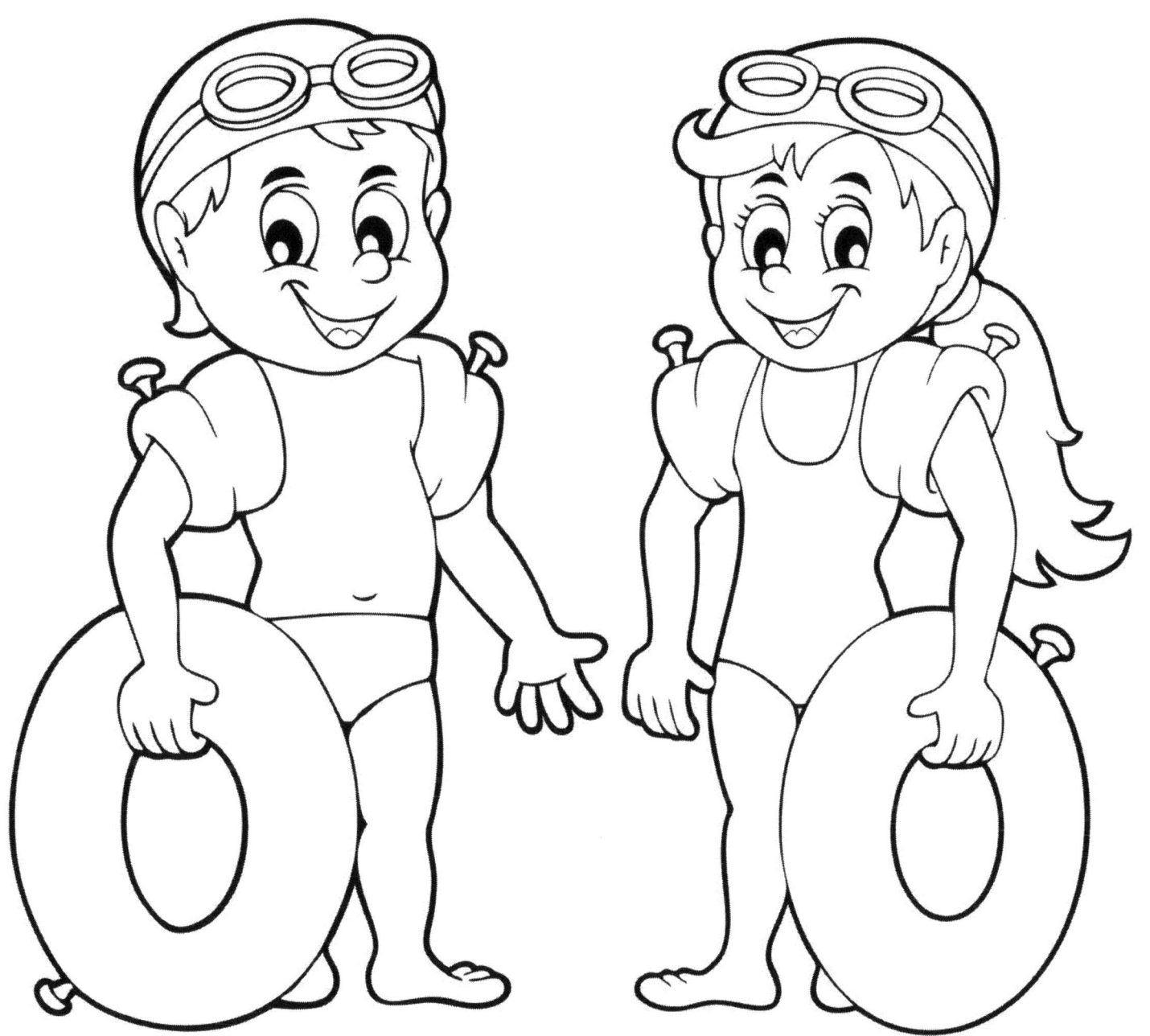

More coloring pages for you to enjoy.

Sports + Activity Coloring Book For Kids — Rachel Mintz

Space and Science Coloring Book For Kids — Rachel Mintz

Princesses Party Coloring Book For Girls — Rachel Mintz

Knights + Castles Coloring Book For Kids — Rachel Mintz

Cars Coloring Book for Kids — Rachel Mintz

Animals Coloring Book For Kids — Rachel Mintz

Guns and Rifles Coloring Book For Kids — Rachel Mintz

Army and Military Coloring Book For Kids — Rachel Mintz

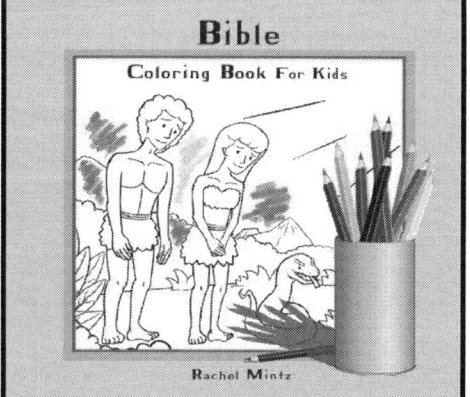

Bible Coloring Book For Kids — Rachel Mintz

More Coloring Books For Kids

New Coloring Books

Did you have fun with this book?
Please let others know by adding a short review at Amazon.
We are thankful for every new review.

Manufactured by Amazon.ca
Bolton, ON

10692417R00057